ABNORMAL PSYCHOLOGY
An introduction to the deviant personality

(Author's note: Proper diagnosis of psychological abnormality must be performed by a trained professional. This book is intended to provide an overview of the many factors which can contribute to such conditions)

The population of mental hospitals peaked in the 1950s with 0.38% of Americans institutionalized. There were more people in hospitals for mental disorders than for all other medical causes combined.

By the 1970s, the old mental retardation classification system had been replaced. Formerly, 75% were classified as morons (IQ 50-70, mental age 7-12); 20% imbeciles (IQ 30-50, mental age 4-7); and 5% idiots (IQ 0-30, mental age 0-4). These antiquated terms are now simply insults.

According to the U.S. Department of Health and Human Services, 80% of the children who die from abuse and neglect are younger than 4 years old, and 20% of children in poverty have a mental health disorder.

Overmedication of children

Globally, the market for psychotropic drugs for children, like antidepressants, antipsychotics and sedatives, is growing 10% per year, with more than $20.7 billion sales for antipsychotics alone. At least 8 million children receive prescriptions for ADD, ADHD, bipolar disorder, autism, depression, schizophrenia, and dozens of other disorders. The diagnosis of ADHD in children is rapidly increasing.

Cultural differences

French child psychiatrists do not use the DSM; they use the CFTMEA (French Classification for Mental Issues in Children and Adolescents). They feel that Americans pathologize what is really normal childish behavior. French children are more rigidly brought up compared to American children. Their meals are at specific times with no snacking between, and babies are allowed to "cry it out" at night rather than being coddled. Behavior limits are enforced, and "no" means exactly that. French parents are in charge of their children, the opposite of what many American families practice.

Current statistics

Some psychiatrists simplistically scan a checklist of symptoms, and then write a prescription, thus omitting an adequate evaluation which should include psychosocial context, pervasiveness, and symptom progress over time which would help distinguish them from merely reaction to life's experiences.

A 2005 New York Times study reported that doctors who accepted payments from pharmaceutical companies for prescribing their drugs were five times more likely to recommend such drugs for children than doctors who didn't.

According to the National Institute for Mental Health (NIMH), at any given time, 18.6% of adult Americans and 20% of teenagers suffer a mental disorder and, over a lifetime, half of us do, yet only 10% of us are in psychotherapy. Men and women suffer equally in numbers, but with different symptoms. Black Americans have 30% less mental illness than white.

80% of the patients report that treatment was effective; 47% received medication without therapy; 34% received both, and 19% received therapy but no medication. Mental disorders are more common than heart disease, cancer, or diabetes, and account for half of all causes of disability.

Deinstitutionalization (replacing hospital confinement with drug therapy) began in the 1960s. Only10% of the mental hospital beds of the 1950s still remain even though our population has doubled. There are three times as many mentally ill persons in jails than in hospitals, mostly for minor offenses like public urination or creating a public disturbance. People with severe mental illness commit only 5% of violent crimes.

Over 90% of suicides are committed by persons with a mental disorder, usually depression or substance abuse. Globally, there are 3000 suicides a day -- a million a year -- and it's rising steadily. 1% of the U.S. population is suicidal with the highest rates between the ages of 18 and 29 years. More women than men consider it, but more men than women do it. One of every 25 attempts is successful -- men by guns, women by prescription drugs.

While it may seem reasonable to blame mental illness for criminal acts, only 7.5% of crimes are committed by persons with severe mental disorders.

Comorbidity:
45% of the population suffers from more than one mental disorder at a given time; for example, depression often accompanies substance abuse and anxicty disorders.

WHAT IS NORMAL?
Virtually everyone displays odd symptoms at times, but more disordered individuals are rigid in their malfunctions, consequently losing friendships and jobs.

"Normal" people have varying degrees of quirkiness that define their personalities. Under stress, these are shared with symptoms seen in a variety of psychiatric disorders such as impulsivity, irritability, aggression, hostility, rage, moodiness, sudden mood changes, agitation, poor concentration, and disorganization.

While smoking, drinking, high productivity, and genius may be "abnormal," they aren't considered a mental health problem unless they cause discomfort, unhappiness, or affect others.

Maladaptation – the inability to reach goals, adapt to the demands of life, or function among others – is the key.

We have a tendency to generalize symptoms, readily name-calling "neurotic" and "paranoid" when those disorders are actually syndromes – clusters of clinically-defined symptoms. Even then, individuals who are inflicted may not display all of the characteristic symptoms.

Not all excessive personality displays indicate pathology; a loud-mouth at a party isn't necessarily a narcissist, but may be merely compensating for a feeling of inferiority, or may be drunk.

The definition of normality varies with the particular group or culture. When defining a baseline for acceptable behavior, or drawing a bell curve for general behavior, children vary wildly up and down from that center line as they experiment with behavior traits, gradually moderating with age and experience.

While constant motion of young children may be distracting to adults, it's necessary as their bodies adjust to their physical growth.

PERSONALITY TRAITS OF NORMAL ADULTS

(***Note:*** *In each of the six trait comparisons, both the category and its oppositional characteristic are considered normal; it is the extremes of these traits that is abnormal*)

1. *Extroversion:* Self esteem and social interaction with a tendency to be active, talkative, optimistic, and affectionate. *Introverts*, on the other hand, tend to prefer solitude and are less active than extroverts; they appear sober, aloof, quiet, task-oriented, and have less need for stimulation.

2. *Openness:* Interested in new experiences, adventurous, imaginative, creative, curious, untraditional; appreciative of the arts, expresses emotion, aware of feelings, may hold unconventional beliefs.

Closed minds are typically more interested in practical, concrete pursuits, are set in their ways and emotionally unresponsive.

3. *Emotional stability:* the ability to remain calm during stressful situations, as opposed to *Neuroticism,* the tendency to experience negative emotions such as anxiety, anger, fear, dependence, depression, and disrupted thinking. They are intolerant of stress, see threats in ordinary situations, exhibit a general bad mood, are pessimistic toward work and personal relations, and have cloudy thinking and decision making. Discontentment increases the likelihood of clinical depression.

4. *Agreeableness:* Compassionate, considerate, trusting and trustworthy, tender-hearted, socially concerned, forgiving, generous, caring, flexible, patiently putting others' needs before themselves, and even appear gullible, willing to compromise, optimistic of human nature.

Disagreeable personalities are likely to be competitive, manipulative, cynical, skeptical, hostile, suspicious, unfriendly, uncooperative, rude, unconcerned with others' well-being, untrusting, and unhelpful.

5. *Conscientiousness:* Self disciplined, ambitious, persistent, dutiful, prudent, strive for perfection, and well planned rather than spontaneous, Conscientiousness rises among young adults, then declines with age.

Low conscientious individuals are less demanding of themselves and others, they are unreliable and careless.

6. *Honest and humble*: Sincere, fair, not greedy, modest.

Maladaptive behavior

Abnormality may be exhibited by four distinct characteristics:

1. *Long Periods of Discomfort*

It is normal to experience discomfort from stress or grief, but this diminishes with time. Persistent discomfort has no reality basis and is abnormal.

2. *Impaired Functioning*

Everyone has periods of inefficiency and moods, but a brilliant person who consistently fails school classes and tasks, or changes jobs for no apparent reason, may need help.

3. *Bizarre Behavior*

Young people experiment with their individuality – piercings, dress style, tattoos, hair coloring – but bizarre behavior like hallucinations (baseless sensory perceptions) or delusions (provably-false beliefs) suggest confusion.

4. *Disruptive Behavior*

Impulsive and apparently uncontrollable behavior disrupts the lives of others or deprives them of their human rights.

Lying

According to popular TV psychiatrist Dr. Phil, the average man lies six times a day and the average woman three times. He lists the following clues to spot a liar. These characteristics are suggestive, not conclusive.

1) Too much or too little eye contact. Liars tend to avoid looking people in the eye, but even if they are staring you down, they may be working hard at lying.

2) Over-emphasizes details or picks some obscure point to emphasize instead of focusing on the key issue.

3) Fidgeting. Is the person you're talking to very fidgety? Kids do this when they're telling a tale.

4) Frequent touching of the nose, face, ear, mouth, throat.

5) Lips tightly closed.

6) Throat clearing, stuttering, hesitating, looking up or down, or other stalling techniques.

7) Answers questions not asked or provide information not needed to defend themselves.

8) Excessive blinking, dilated pupils, voice pitch changes, less smiling, shrugging shoulders, crossed arms.

9) Shaking head while making a point (Even Dr. Phil does this during his telecasts).

10) Too rehearsed. They've got a story and they'll repeat key phrases over and over.

11) They don't like saying "I" or "me" because they don't want to own the lie, so they may say "It didn't happen" instead of "I didn't do it."

12) Liars are repetitive. When you ask, "Did you drive over there last night?" they may answer, "I did not drive over there last night."

13) Liars often avoid contractions in their speech and are overly emphatic: "I did not do that!"

Specific Learning Disorder (SLD)

As many as 1 out of every 5 people in the United States has a life-long learning disability. 1 million school children receive special education in school; one third of those show reading disability (dyslexia – the largest percentage), mathematics disability (dyscalculia), and writing disability (dysgraphia). They are not "dumb" or "lazy;" their brains sinply process information differently, so they may:

- have trouble learning the alphabet, rhyming words, or connecting letters to their sounds;
- make many mistakes when reading aloud, and repeat and pause often;
- not understand what they read;
- have real trouble with spelling;

- have very messy handwriting or hold a pencil awkwardly;
- struggle to express ideas in writing;
- learn language late and have a limited vocabulary;
- have trouble remembering the sounds that letters make or hearing slight differences between words;
- have trouble understanding jokes, comic strips, and sarcasm;
- have trouble following directions;
- mispronounce words or use a wrong word that sounds similar;
- have trouble organizing what they want to say or not be able to think of the word they need to write or say;
- not follow the social rules of conversation, such as taking turns, and stand too close to the listener;
- confuse math symbols and misread numbers;
- not be able to retell a story in order of events;
- not know how to begin a task or how to continue from there.

Types of Mental Disorders (Approximate percentage in the U.S. adult population; fluctuates over time and by poll)

Acute stress disorder (distress resulting from exposure to an event)

Adjustment disorder

Alcoholism (6%; young men 21%)

Amnesia

Anxiety disorders (18.1% of adults)

Separation anxiety lasting more than six months

Panic disorder (2.7% of adults)

Phobias (10.5% of adults)

Post-traumatic stress disorder (PTSD) (3.5% of adults; 20-30% of veterans)

Selective mutism

General anxiety disorder (3.1% of adults)

Behavioral disorders
    Attention deficit hyperactivity disorder (ADHD) (4.1% of adults))
    Conduct disorder
    Oppositional defiant disorder
Communication disorders
    Language disorder (receptive-expressive language disorder)
    Speech sound disorder (formerly called phonological disorder)
    Childhood-onset fluency disorder (stuttering)
    Social-pragmatic communication disorder (difficulties in verbal and non-verbal communication)
Developmental disorders
    Intellectual disability (formerly called mental retardation)
    Learning disorders
    Autism (1+%) (4:1 boys:girls; Asperger syndrome 10:1 boys:girls)
Dissociative disorders
    Dissociative amnesia
    Dissociative identity disorder (DID) (formerly called multiple personality)
Eating disorders (4%)
    Anorexia nervosa (0.6% of adults)
    Bulimia (1% of adults)
    Binge eating disorder (2.8% of adults)
    Pica and rumination disorder
Gender identity disorder
    Homosexuality
    Transvestism
    Transexuality
    Hermaphrodism (Intersex)
    Pseudohermaphrodism

Asexuality
Impulse control disorders
Kleptomania
Pyromania
Gambling addiction
Intermittent explosive disorder (IED)
Trichotillomania (hair pulling)
Mood disorders (9.5% of adults)
Major depressive disorder (excluding bereavement)
(formerly called nervous breakdown; 6.7% of adults)
Dysthymic disorder (Mild, chronic depression) (1.5% of
adults)
Bipolar disorder (formerly called manic depressive)
(2.6% of adults)
Cyclothymic disorder
Motor disorders
Developmental coordination disorder
Stereotypic movement disorder
Tourette's disorder (0.8%)
Tic disorder
Neurocognitive disorders
Dementia and amnesia
Obsessive-compulsive disorder (OCD)
Body dysmorphic disorder (preoccupied with flaws in
appearance)
Hoarding disorder
Excoriation (skin picking) disorder
Paraphilias
Pedophilia
Voyeurism
Exhibitionism
Fetishism
Frotteurism
Sexual masochism

Sexual sadism
Transvestitism
Personality disorders (9.1% of adults)
Paranoid personality disorder (5%)
Schizoaffective disorder
Schizoid personality disorder (3%)
Schizotypal personality disorder (3%)
Antisocial personality disorder (psychopathy, sociopathy) (1% of adults)
Borderline personality disorder (2% of adults, mostly young women)
Histrionic personality disorder (2%)
Narcissistic personality disorder (3% age 65+, 10% age 20s)
Avoidant personality disorder (5% of adults)
Dependent personality disorder (0.5%)
Psychotic disorders (2%-3%)
Schizophrenia (1.1% of adults)
Brief psychotic disorder
Delusional disorder
Shared psychotic disorder
Substance-induced psychotic disorder
Sleep disorders (13%)
Insomnia
Narcolepsy
Hypersomnia
Somatoform disorders
Somatization disorder
Conversion disorder
Pain disorder
Undifferentiated somatoform disorder
Illness anxiety disorder (formerly called hypochondriasis)

Suicide (.01% of adults, 90% of whom have a mental disorder, usually depression or substance abuse)

"Quirky" personalities

With so many variables in personality, it's hard to pinpoint abnormality. The "enforcer" could be a vigilante, a law man, or a hall monitor. The drama queen can create quite a scene for no apparent reason at all. The hoarder just can't throw anything away. And the shopaholic can't resist a shopping mall.

Neurosis or Psychosis?

A neurotic individual recognizes that he has a problem and often possesses nervous habits like severe tics, excessive smoking or drinking, obsessive/compulsive behavior, phobias, or panic. Psychotic symptoms, however, involve altered perceptions, thoughts, or consciousness. These delusions and hallucinations arise from disordered thinking. Their "reality" is actually a fantasy.

Psychoses

Organic brain disorders: Delirium or shock-like symptoms include frequent breaks in attention, memory impairment, incoherent speech, and may have a distorted sense of time and space.

Alcohol and drug abuse: Chronic use of hallucinatory or psychotropic drugs, and stimulants ("uppers") like methamphetamine ("speed") produce disordered thought, extreme anxiety, hallucinations, and paranoia.

Some of these symptoms can be attributed to lack of sleep over extended periods. Chronic alcoholics often display psychosis when extremely intoxicated or when withdrawing from drinking (delirium tremens).

Bi-polar disorder *(formerly manic depressive):* When in the manic state, a person displays unrealistic and unobtainable plans or goals. Such delusions of grandeur along with a distinct lack of judgment result in inappropriate public behavior such as untoward sexual advances, dominating conversations, excessive drinking or drug use. Little sleep is required in the manic state.

Schizophrenia (formerly called dementia praecox): Hallucinations (especially auditory) and delusions are characteristic of this chronic mental disorder which normally begins in childhood, often at age 6, and worsens over time. The schizophrenic has difficulty processing information correctly.

This psychotic condition affects 1% of the population, and 47% of the siblings of a schizophrenic. Three million Americans live in an imaginary world, dissociated from reality. Fifty percent of hospitalized mental care patients have schizophrenia, 1.5 times more men than women. Historically called "mad," "loony," "crazy," "insane," or "maniac" (not "manic *"*).

Schizophrenia is not a violent illness; the odds of being murdered by a schizophrenic stranger is 1 in 14.3 million, 1/3 the likelihood of being killed by lightning.

Symptoms

Delusion: Misperception of reality. They often invent or preach, and may exhibit "word salad" (an array of unconnected words).

Paranoia: May feel either persecuted (believes he is malevolently or unfairly treated) or grandiose ("delusions of grandeur;"). They have an inflated self-worth, power, or knowledge because they believe they have a special relationship with a famous person, deity, another high-status individual, or that he is that high-status person.

They may have auditory hallucinations, but normal intellect and affect, and may exhibit anger, aloofness, and anxiety. He may find personal references in others' behavior, writings, and broadcasts.

Hallucinations: Imaginary excitation of any of the senses, most typically auditory (hearing voices that comment on or urge behavior, issue orders, or accuse of violent actions. A non-psychotic form may be *dissociation,* a psychological separation from a reality that is too painful to process consciously, accompanied by a retreat into an imaginary world.

Illusions: Misperception of a real stimulus, as in "optical (visual) illusion."

Disorganized, bizarre speech and behavior: Sudden, unpredictable and inappropriate actions, speech, writing, or behavior due to fragmentary delusions or hallucinations.

Flat affect: (no eye contact, expressionless, apathy, monotone, unemotional); poverty of speech (short response, slow speech); loss of directedness (slow movement, unable to initiate, non-socialization)

Catatonic: Motor immobility or excessive, purposeless mobility; resists instructions to move or speak, but may be manually positioned; repeats words or movements of others.

Undifferentiated: Meets general schizophrenic definition, but not the subtypes.

Schizoaffective: A comorbidity combining major mood disorder with psychosis.

*   *   *   *

PARANOID SCHIZOPHRENIA
A Case Study

Steven is a 50 year old truck driver from the Midwest, formerly a military communications technician who contacted me because I had sophisticated electronic equipment to perform an electronic body scan. He admitted to early bad behavior that put him in jail, but says he is now a born-again Christian.

He says the symptoms started after he split with his wife. One day he ached all over and couldn't get up for four days. He heard a voice outside his mobile home and wondered if he was losing his mind, but said no, he doesn't see and hear things.

The voice was probably female, and from an organized group. The messages are more conceptual than clearly audible; he calls this "sonic enhancement." Sometimes there are different voices, and occasionally several at once, as though in conference.

They wake him often during the night and ask him very personal and general questions, as well as vulgar and derogatory things. They talk to him about the word of God, events, science and history, and know private things about his family.

Steven reports no family history of psychological problems, but is currently being medicated for high blood pressure and gastric acidity. He also admits to a brief attempt to have psychiatric counseling that "didn't get anywhere."

He suspected that some agency implanted a device on his body that enables them to hear everything he says. Even if he reads, they know what he's reading because of what he calls "sub-vocalization" (minor lip movements as he reads words to himself).

He claims he did a lot of on-line research, and has been to V.A. hospitals for MRI and CAT scans as well as ultrasound, and that his neck and spine have been X-rayed 15 times with nothing found.

He also says he had taken anti-psychotic drugs which didn't help his condition. He says he is angry that they have done this to him, and they won't tell him why.

"They said they were here to help me because of someone I did something for in the past. But I have no private moments and I'm very frustrated."

"What makes you think you had an implant?"

"I have pain, hear voices, my teeth vibrate, and my right ear and neck go numb."

"Do you have any scars on your body that are unaccountable?

"No."

"Who do you think implanted the device?"

"The FBI, DEA, NIMH, or Geospatial Intelligence Agency."

At this point I did do an electronic sweep to find any implanted device; there was no indication of metal. He then said that the implant was all plastic except for tiny electrical contacts.

Next, I employed instruments to detect radio emissions, again with no response.

"How often do you hear these voices?" I asked.

"All the time."

"Are you hearing them now?"

"Yes."

"What are they saying?"

"That you seem to be a nice enough fellow, very qualified in electronics, but that you will never find the device because it's too small."

I asked him if he could forward some questions to them,

"Just ask them; they can hear everything you say."

I asked where the device was on his body.

"They won't say; it's sub dermal."

What frequency does it operate on?

"They won't say that, either."

"Why not?"

"Because if you knew the frequency, you could find the other devices."

"How many people have these devices implanted in them?"

"Sixteen. Not exactly sixteen, that's just a number. They don't want to reveal how many there are."

"Are they controlling this from the U.S.?"

"Yes."

"Nearby?"

"No."

"From a satellite?"

"Yes."

I then asked where they are located, and he said they wouldn't tell him, but in the U.S. and Mexico.

"Now they are saying they aren't part of the U.S. Government, and they are very interested in what you do. They are a consortium of many, bound by a common good. They want me to talk about my new inventions like a perpetual motion engine that uses no fuel and gives off no emissions."

I asked them if they spoke other languages like German.

"Yes; what do you want to ask them?

"Ich weiss nicht," I answered.

"You don't know?" was his correct reply.

Steven admitted he was based in Germany and knew the language.

I asked if they knew about classical music; the answer was yes.

"How many symphonies did Brahms and Mendelssohn write?"

The responses were completely wrong. Steven then said they preferred country and rock, so I didn't investigate that subject any further.

At the end of the session, I recommended that he resume counseling and prescription medications to eliminate any question that the voices had a psychological origin.

I also suggested he find an electronics manufacturer that had a Faraday Cage (screen room) that would prevent radio waves from entering. He could go in and out of that room to see if the voices stopped while he was inside, and resumed as he came back out.

He thanked me for the interview and said he would be in touch with me regarding his progress. I received an email about nine months later saying that things were about the same. Subsequent attempts to contact him have failed.

*   *   *   *

GENESIS OF DISORDERS
Mental disorders may be functional (psychogenic or pyschosocial), arising from experiences, attitudes, or social roles, or organic (amentia) if present at birth. The latter may be hereditary (genetogenic), exaggerated by inbreeding; congenital if it develops after conception; chemogenic if it arises from an imbalance in body chemistry like hormones; or somatogenic if anatomically induced by tumors, injury, structure, or illness.

SEASONAL EFFECTS
Because of the shorter time of daylight as measured by our biological clocks, people born in winter months have a higher risk of disorders including winter depression (seasonal affective disorder), bipolar depression, and schizophrenia.

PHENOTYPES (Appearance)
Down's syndrome (Mongolism): Body stocky and squat, eyes slanted, protruding thick tongue, short fingers, thumb separated, toes spread. IQ 50-70, life span typically to middle adolescence, extra 21st chromosome. Mother usually had a late-age pregnancy.
Cretin: Short, dwarf-like, with a thyroid deficiency.
Hydrocephalic ("water on the brain"): Fluid compresses the brain, damaging its development; skull is expanded, exhibiting a very large head.
Microcephalic ("pinhead"): Underdeveloped brain.

TREATMENT OPTIONS, historical and current
Euthanasia: "Mercy killing" of the insane, criminals, aged, non-self-sufficient.
Sterilization: Sexual neutering to prevent passing on hereditary characteristics.
Institutionalization: Assign the afflicted to wards, prisons and medical facilities.
Rehabilitation: Education and training to enhance skills.
Surgery: Correction of physical disorder.
Chemotherapy: Medication to treat the disorder.
Counseling: Cognitive therapy, especially helpful if the disorder is not organic.

The Rorschach Test

Rorschach developed his test in 1921, using hundreds of random ink blots of various combinations and colors which he showed to hundreds of patients and normal control subjects, recording their interpretations. He finally settled on the best ten which showed the greatest consistency in responses from the control group and variability among the mental subjects.

Originally intended to diagnose schizophrenia, its use has grown for its variety of diagnostic indicators. Each card looks for specific responses, but differ among various cultures.

AUTISM SPECTRUM DISORDER (Now includes Asperger's syndrome)

Warning signs in babies: By age 6 months they don't smile; by 12 months they don't point, wave, or babble; and by 16 months they speak no words at all.

Prevalence: 1 in 54 boys; less in girls. There is no credible evidence that autism is on the increase, only that previously-misidentified symptoms are now being assigned to autism spectrum disorder.

Autistic children typically:
1. Won't respond to their names
2. Don't wave "bye-bye."
3. Tune people out rather than integrate with them
4. Are uninterested in other children
5. Have poor eye contact

Autistic symptoms present from early childhood:
1. Few relationships, due to abnormal or minimal social approach, and poor conversational skills as well as nonverbal communication like eye contact, body language, facial expression, and gestures.

2. Inability to make and keep friendships because of an apparent absence of interest in people.

3. Repetitive patterns of behavior, speech, interests, or activities, displayed as motor movements, use of objects, and immediate repetition of words said by others (echolalia)> Repetitive behavior is also found in obsessive-compulsive disorder (OCD), Parkinson's disease, and Tourette syndrome.

4. Rigid adherence to routines and rejection of change and ritualized verbal or nonverbal behavior. Intensely fixated on unusual subjects or objects.

5. Hyper- or hypo-reactive senses of pain, heat, cold, specific sounds, or textures.

6. Obsessive smelling, touching, lining up patterns of objects.

7. Fascination with lights or spinning objects.

Autism runs in families and may be detected as young as one year old. Autistic individuals lack empathy and they don't understand people, but they are good at making sense out of the physical world which they view with detachment.

`Those with lower IQ may exhibit obsession, often staring for long periods at something, or memorizing license plates or posted schedules.

Usually, a normal one-year-old, when presented with a new toy, will typically eye it with interest, raise his eyebrows, and face the adult, then reach out and ask for it with a short vocalization.

In contrast, the autistic child may stare at the toy, but won't reach for it or look at the adult. If given that toy, they will home in on it, playing with it endlessly.

Poor motor control – timed movements – results in poor handwriting in autistic children. Character size, alignment, and spacing are normal, but coordination for forming letters is deficient.

Autistic children throw long temper tantrums as a result of their inability to communicate. They scream instead of talk and become increasingly violent. In the more severe examples, they may repetitively shout words or noises (echolalia), rock their bodies back and forth, flap their hands, or even flail their arms or legs.

The cause of autism is unknown; it affects only 0.2% of the population, and is far more prevalent in boys than girls (10:1 for Asperger's). Gender may be a clue, since males are more direct and physical, while females are more indirect and verbal, and have better social skills.

Asperger's Syndrome

Formerly a separate category, it is now combined with autism because of similar traits, even though there are significant neurological differences as shown on an electroencephalograph (EEG).

AS is high-intellect autism, displaying good systemization skills, but difficulty with social skills, communication, motor skills, and sensory responses.

Obsessively driven in a narrow, detailed focus, "Aspies" are often considered "nerds" or "geeks" who, from an early age, relentlessly and competently pursue science, mathematics, engineering, computer programming, mechanics, art, or writing. Many scientists and academics are thought to have AS.

They consider language an informational exchange, not a social contact, so they often monopolize long-winded conversations as well as postal mail or email, even if the listener or recipient tries to change the subject, or they may not talk at all.

Choice of words or delivery may seem inappropriately formal or informal, and delivered monotonously, rigidly, or unusually fast.

Since they are autistic, Asperger's subjects lack eye contact or facial expression; often move awkwardly, clumsily bumping into things.

They appear not to understand or empathize with others' feelings, and have a difficult time "reading" other people or understanding humor. They don't easily take redirection by others.

Since their sensory systems are often over- or under-sensitive; an AS subject may become very agitated in crowds, and react to lighting, smell, and taste differently from other people.

ADD/ADHD

Attention Deficit Hyperactivity Disorder is a symptomatic cluster of three primary characteristics which must persist for at least six months:

Inattention: Disorganized, bored, easily distracted, and frequently lost in daydreams. Makes careless mistakes and doesn't follow instructions. Underestimates time to do tasks, often late, and tends to procrastinate. May appear aloof or arrogant due to inattentiveness. May show obsessive interest in subjects of interest like cars, video games, music, or sports, ignoring uninteresting subjects.

Impulsivity: Restless, fidgety, incessant talks and switches subjects; feels overwhelmed.

Hyperactivity: If present (ADHD), subject may be impatient, irritable, reactive, outspoken, interruptive.

These characteristics may start by age 12, but sometimes not until adulthood, and are observable in more than one setting (classroom, playground, social, home, community), and is impairing.

Only one in seven adults with ADD (attention deficit without the hyperactivity) is aware they have it. Medication improves 80% of the cases. Comorbidity of ADHD with autism spectrum disorder is possible.

The cause may be chemical imbalance between neurons, unable to fire in the messaging system unless intense interest is present.

Recent studies suggest that physical movement like leg swinging, chair wiggling, and squirming might be necessary for them to work out complex cognitive tasks, and that suppressing these movements might actually obstruct their learning.

It is the most commonly studied and diagnosed psychiatric disorder in children (5% in the U.S., 0.5% in France). At least half of these children will carry their symptoms into adulthood.

Close observation is required for accurate diagnosis, since similar symptoms can be triggered by depression, death or divorce in the family, lack of sleep, abuse, hearing loss, learning disability, or seizures.

American child psychiatrists suspect biological causes, but French psychotherapists believe it is social and situational, and treat it with counseling.

SAVANT SYNDROME (formerly called "idiot" savant)

This individual possesses below-normal intelligence, but has a special talent or ability in a specific area, usually mathematics, music, or visual arts.

Social and communicative skills are lacking, often severely, and are present by ages 5-6.

Roughly 50% of children who display this are also autistic; correspondingly,10% of autistic children are savants. The anatomical cause is not known. One theory suggests that a damaged left hemisphere of the brain is being overcompensated by the right hemisphere.

The most common skill is extraordinary data memorization of sports statistics, population figures, and historical or biographical information. A popularized performance is quickly reciting the day of the week for a specific historical or future date. This skill generally improves with age and practice.

Mathematical savant Daniel Tammet recited pi (3.14...) to over 20,000 decimal places.

Musical savants often have perfect pitch and can play a piece perfectly after hearing it performed just once.

STOCKHOLM SYNDROME

In 1973 a Stockholm, Sweden, bank employee became romantically attached to a robber who held her hostage. Long-term abductions impose intimidation, threats, and even brutality which keeps its victim in a perpetual state of fear, thus becoming obsessed with pacifying and pleasing the captor.

This obedience of fear and dependence is also present in some domestic situations, inducing a dominant/submissive type of relationship, engendering affection for survival, physically and emotionally.

MUNCHAUSEN SYNDROME ("Hospital Addiction," "Hospital Hopper," "Malingering")

This contrived disorder is characterized by an individual who feigns an illness or injury in order to draw attention or sympathy.

Munchausen Syndrome by Proxy: Most commonly a mother (occasionally a health-care provider) feigns sickness in a healthy child in order to draw attention or sympathy to her. She might invent symptoms, contaminate a urine test, falsify medical records, or induce symptoms by poisoning, suffocating, starving, or intentionally infecting the victim.

Perpetrators seem very friendly, cooperative, and overly-concerned with the patient who has had many hospitalizations.

Characteristics often include:

1. A strange set of symptoms, reportedly worse than or different from those observed by medical personnel;

2. Other similar illnesses reported in the family;

3. Improvement in the hospital but recurrent symptoms at home;

4. Non-matching blood samples provided;

5. Chemicals detected in the blood, stool, or urine.

KORSAKOFF'S SYNDROME

Memory loss produced by chronic alcoholism causes a reduction of vitamin B1 (thiamin), consequently damaging or destroying nerve cells, thus resulting in dementia, psychosis, and unsteady movements similar to drunkenness.

PHOBIAS: Irrational or exaggerated, specific fears lasting more than six months
(See full list of 600 at http://phobialist.com/index.html*)*

Claustrophobia: Fear of enclosed spaces
Agoraphobia: Fear of crowded places
Arachnophobia: Fear of spiders
Merinthophobia: Fear of being bound or tied up
Acrophobia: Fear of heights
Gephyrophobia: Fear of crossing bridges
Verminophobia: Fear of germs
Xenophobia: Fear of strangers
Triskaidekaphobia: Fear of the number 13
Paraskavedekatriaphobia: Fear of Friday the 13th
Cyberphobia: Fear of computers
Pteronophobia: Fear of being tickled by feathers

Phobophobia: Fear of acquiring a phobia
Coulrophobia: Fear of clowns
Metamfiezomaiophobia: Fear of mimes
Pupphobia: Fear of puppets
Ecclesiophobia: Fear of church
Bogypobia: Fear of the bogeyman
Omphalophobia: Fear of belly buttons
Caligynephobia: Fear of beautiful women
Parthenophobia: Fear of virgins
Peladophobia: Fear of bald people
Gerontophobia: Fear of old people
Hexakosioihexekontahexaphobia: Fear of the number 666

Most Unpleasant Sounds (Rated from 74 different sounds)
The most unpleasant noises were high pitched, least unpleasant
were low pitched:

(Most unpleasant)	(Least unpleasant)
Knife on a bottle	Applause
Fork on a glass	Baby laughing
Chalk on a blackboard	Thunder
Ruler tapping a bottle	Water flowing
Fingernails on a blackboard	
Female scream	
Baby crying	
Electric drill	

PARAPHILIAS: DEVIANT SEXUAL ARROUSAL
Sexual gratification between men and women is a natural
biological mechanism for perpetuation of the species; deviant
gratification is not.
Fetishism: Use of objects for gratification.
Transvestism: Cross-dressing.
Sadism and masochism: Giving or receiving painful humiliation.
Voyeurism: Spying on others who may be naked or having sex.
Frotteurism: Rubbing up against others in a crowd, unnoticed.
Exhibitionist: Males who expose their genitals in public.
Pedophilia: Sexual contact with children.

GENDER IDENTITY DISORDERS
Hypersexuality: Excessive sexual urges.
Homosexuality: Sexual preference for partners of the same
gender; gay or Lesbian
Transgender (transsexual): Gender identity different from
physical sexual assignment; not homosexuality

Hermaphrodism (intersexual): Anatomical presence of both male and female genitalia.

Pseudohermaphrodism: Deficiency of the hormone 17-B-hydroxysteroid dehydrogenase (17-B-HSD) during pregnancy leaves male reproductive organs deformed and buried deep within their abdomens.

At birth, they are misidentified as girls because genitalia appear to be female; but at puberty, testosterone generation results in facial hair and increasingly masculine features. Gender transformation surgery is applied.

Bisexuality: Sexual attraction toward both males and females.

Gender queer: Doesn't feel either male or female roles and stereotypes, including dress

Asexuality: Feels no sexual attraction to either gender, or has no desire to act on such feelings.

ATTITUDES

Cynic: Believes that only selfishness motivates human actions, ignoring, dismissing, or minimizing selfless acts.

Skeptic: Questions the validity or authenticity of something purporting to be factual.

Optimist: Usually expects a favorable outcome.

Pessimist: Habitually sees or anticipates the worst, or is disposed to be gloomy.

Realist: Tends to view or represent things as they really are.

Pragmatist: Practical; oriented toward the success or failure of an action or a thought.

Passive-Aggressive: Aggression expressed unassertively as stubbornness, uncommunicative, procrastination.

DISRUPTIVE IMPULSE CONTROL AND CONDUCT DISORDERS

Oppositional defiant disorder: Subdivided into angry/irritable mood, argumentative/defiant behavior, and vindictiveness. Key factors include severity and presence under a variety of settings. In children, this may be normal when incidental.

Conduct disorder: Callous and unemotional relationships in various settings.

Addictive disorder: Activates the brain reward system; includes craving, intoxication, and withdrawal. It may be induced by substance abuse like illicit drugs, alcohol, nicotine, cannabis, caffeine, or by an activity like gambling.

Conversion disorder (Hysteria): Presents as a physical disability (sensory or motor), or violent emotional outbreaks, but is actually mentally induced (autosuggestion) by anxiety and has no anatomical cause. Examples include glove anesthesia, mutism, deafness, blindness, skin insensitivity, vertigo, paralysis, and tremors.

Hypochondria: An excessive preoccupation with one's health, usually focusing on one specific symptom.

Mania: Excessively driven and enthusiastic, energetic and competitive, confident and creative, they want to "change the world." It is common among immigrants who are restless to "get up and go somewhere else," thus leading to their American entrepreneurial reputation. They can be overconfident, irritable, and impulsive. Unlike narcissists, hypomanics (lower-level mania) can be knocked down a notch.

Famous Hypomanics:

Christopher Columbus: Claimed he'd discovered the Garden of Eden and believed he was destined to usher in the apocalypse.

Andrew Carnegie: The richest man in the world, tried to stop World War I by building peace temples throughout Europe.

George Patton: Corrected historians based on his "memory" of famous battles he'd fought in past lives.

Jim Clark: Founder of Silicon Graphics and Netscape, he started Healtheon, a company he predicted would solve the American health care crisis. It didn't.

Rahm Immanuel (Obama's initial chief of staff) ruled his roost with a profane whip.

Impulse Control Disorder (ICD): Anxiety can only be relieved by some defined behavior pattern.

Intermittent explosive disorder: "Hot-headedness;" fFrequent physical or verbal outbursts, discounting youthful temper tantrums and ADHD.

Pathological gambling: persistent and recurrent maladaptive gambling behavior that disrupts personal, family, or vocational pursuits.

Kleptomania: Must steal an item even though it isn't needed or wanted.

Eating Disorders:

Bulimia nervosa: Eating, then forcing vomiting.

Anorexia nervosa: Self-imposed starvation; may include bulimia, and has the highest death rate of any mental disorder.

Binge eating

Pica: Eating non-foods.

Hoarding Disorder: The hoarder can't bear to throw anything away; they might need it someday. Piles of newspapers and magazines, clothes, cans of food, even pets accumulate in huge, unmanageable lots.

Hoarders can be perfectionists and neat freaks as well, and are paralyzed by the thought that they can't overcome it. There is clinical evidence of abnormal brain activity in the hoarder. At least four million Americans fully qualify for this diagnosis.

Tics: A common, repetitive habit which gives a feeling of satisfaction. Examples include tongue and lip movements, sighing, yawning, throat clearing, biting a lip or inside cheek, sniffing, fiddling, crossing legs, nail biting, nose picking, blinking, shuffling feet, scratching and picking, stretching eyelids, hair twirling/pulling/chewing. They are usually representative of emotional conflicts, but harmless.

BIPOLAR DISORDER (Formerly manic-depressive disorder): Extreme high/low mood swings, typically beginning at age 19. Without long-term observation, roughly half of BPD cases are misdiagnosed as depression, schizophrenia, borderline personality disorder, or substance abuse.

When manic, afflicted individuals may have 1000 great ideas a minute and must tell everybody. They are uncontrollably ebullient or irritable, restless, and have an exaggerated self-image of power, importance and ability, with grandiose solutions to the world's problems. They consider friends and relatives who don't acknowledge and agree with their wisdom as traitors and enemies.

When the mood switches to deep depression, diminished drive, guilt, and despair, they may be suicidal. They lose interest in activities, and become lethargic and fatigued.

The condition is best treated with psychotherapy, although antipsychotic drugs and mood stabilizers can stabilize anxiety and reactivity during the manic and depressive states.

ISSOCIATIVE IDENTITY DISORDER (DID) *Formerly multiple personality disorder (MPD)*

Popularly known as "split personality," often attributed to traumatic childhood experience from which they "dissociate" (remove from conscience), DID affects 3% of the population, and nine times more women than men. These individuals assume alternative identities which may or may not be aware of each other.

Each identity may have its own emotions, pulse, blood pressure, and blood flow to the brain as well as totally different wardrobes, possessions, interests, religions, ages, sexual orientation, value systems, speech patterns, accents, and even right- or left-handedness.

Some therapists question whether DID actually exists or is a culture-based myth – merely excessive suggestibility. Some individuals who may benefit legally or emotionally pretend to have it. U.S. cases far outnumber other countries.

Inaccurately-portrayed dramas like *The Three Faces of Eve* and *Sybil* misidentify real clinical symptoms which include:

1. Dissociation (lapses in memory from significant life events, like birthdays, wedding, or birth of a child;

2. Blackouts in time, resulting in finding oneself in places, but not recalling how one traveled there;

3. Frequent accusations of lying when being told of things they did but do not recall;

4. Finding items in one's possession, but not recalling how they were acquired;

5. Being called by names they don't recognize;

6. Finding writings they have done, but in handwriting other than their own;

7. Hearing voices inside their head that are not their own;

8. Not recognizing themselves in the mirror;

9. Derealization (feeling unreal);

10. Feeling like they are watching themselves move through life rather than living their own life; and

11. Feeling like more than one person.

PERSONALITY DISORDERS

NOTE: Some personality disorders have been rearranged in the DSM-V, including narcissism. The new dimensional approach consists of making an overall, general diagnosis of personality disorder for a given patient, and then selecting particular traits from a long list in order to best describe that specific patient. This is in contrast to the prototype approach that has been used for the past 30 years whereby the narcissistic syndrome is defined by a cluster of related traits, and the clinician matches patients to that profile.

* * * *

While functional disorders like mood, anxiety or delusion affect the afflicted individual, personality disorders affect others as well. The difference is often a matter of degree and rigidity. There are some professions in which personality disorders are actually advantageous, such as the narcissistic celebrity.

Approximately 10% of the adult population and 30% of mental health patients exhibit one or more of the ten traditional personality disorders which include long-standing patterns of maladaptive behavior or improper or immature responses to problems or situations.

These inflexible patterns of perceiving, reacting, and relating to other people and events, impairs their ability to function socially. Since these individuals do not feel like they are doing anything wrong, they see no reason to change their behavior.

Cluster A: Odd or eccentric personality disorder (withdrawn; often reclusive, cold, suspicious, irrational)

Paranoid: Distrusting, and suspecting malevolent motives from others, they are preoccupied with unjustified doubts, including fidelity of their spouses, and excessively trust their own knowledge and abilities to avoid close relationships.

They read hidden, demeaning, or threatening messages in innocent remarks, and present as cold and distant. They are humorless, shift blame to others, and persistently bear grudges.

Schizoid: This loner is solitary and friendless by preference, avoids relationships, is frigid emotionally and sexually, is indifferent to praise or criticism, and does not desire popularity.

They seek jobs requiring little social contact and appear humorless and distant.

Schizotypal: They may have a mild case of, or precursor to, schizophrenia. Cold and aloof, they consistently exhibit odd behavior and beliefs like magical thinking, odd appearance, thinking, and speech (overly elaborate, difficult to follow).

They may exhibit paranoia, excessive social anxiety, belief in having supernatural powers, and think that unrelated events somehow do relate to them.

They lack close friends and have difficulty concentrating for long periods, and may experience hallucinations, illusions, and delusions.

Cluster B: Dramatic, emotional or erratic personality disorder (attention seeking; unpredictable, noticeable behavior)

Antisocial Personality Disorder (APD): Characterized by lack of empathy or conscience, a difficulty controlling impulses, and manipulative behaviors. Also called psychopathy or sociopathy, but Antisocial Personality Disorder is the clinical terminology. *(An expansive overview follows later)*

Borderline Personality Disorder (BPD): Originally named because characteristics border between neurosis and psychosis. 75% are women (mostly young) with separation anxiety (terrified of being abandoned) and need presence of others for self-definition.

As children they are hypersensitive, emotional, highly reactive, and hard to control. They think in black-and-white terms, no gray areas, and have intense but unstable, stormy, conflict-ridden relationships with friends, family, and romantic partners.

They are quick to anger when expectations aren't met, and over-reactive to what they consider affronts. They do have compassion toward others and want a happy relationship.

The BPD is inappropriately hostile, dysfunctional, insecure, verbally abusive, depressed, lonely, has drastic mood swings which can last for hours, and bouts of anger which can spiral out of control, which can result in self-mutilation or (rarely) suicide.

They are self-loathing, self-destructive, even manipulatively suicidal over minor incidents.

Other characteristics include impulsive buying, gambling, substance abuse, strong sexuality, and elevated drive. They suffer from chronic boredom, emptiness, and periods of stress-related paranoia and dissociative symptoms. It is often misdiagnosed as bipolar disorder.

Histrionic Personality Disorder (HPD): Excessively shallow emotionally, these "drama queens" can be very theatrical in action and speech, using flowery language to describe everyday events. Mostly female, and common among actresses constantly seeking attention, they can't really connect.

They need to be the center of attention, often interrupting others to dominate the conversation. They require excessive reassurance and approval, and exhibit temper outbursts if ignored. They are manipulative, superficial, naïve, insincere, and highly suggestible.

Attractive appearance is important, and they may dress seductively. Exaggerated feelings and illnesses are expressed to gain attention. Serial romances, exaggerated interpretation of friendships, and a belief that everyone loves them, are typical.

Narcissistic Personality Disorder (NPD): Like the mythological Greek Narcissus who fell in love with his own reflection in a pond, the narcissist is in love with his imaginary image. He feels entitled to favored treatment and adulation because he feels special and unique.

Flow chart of evolving narcissism:
Pride > arrogance > egotism > egomania > megalomania > narcissism > malignant narcissism (psychopathy/sociopathy)
(An expansive overview of narcissism follows later)

Cluster C: Anxious, fearful

Avoidant Personality Disorder: While most people are understandably cautious, the avoidant personality goes to the extreme to shun closeness and avert rejection, and avoids risk taking to escape the humiliation of failure.

Since social inhibition and anxiety create feelings of inadequacy, low self-esteem, and repressed self-confidence, they exaggerate neutral or slightly-negative interpersonal experiences, and prefer jobs with little social contact. Potential difficulties of new situations are exaggerated to rationalize avoiding them.

They yearn for close friends, but are unwilling to get involved unless there is certainty of being liked, and they may fantasize to avoid the real world.

Dependent Personality Disorder: These individuals need to be taken care of and are indecisive without excessively seeking help, letting others make decisions for them. Usually women over 40, they were probably over-protected as children.

They appear meek, submissive, agreeable, clinging, affectionate, and admiring in order to hold on to others, even abusive partners, and quickly acquire a new relationship at the termination of a former one.

They have difficulty initiating projects, making decisions, and expressing disagreement. They are preoccupied with fear of being left alone, and may be suicidal when rejected, feeling hopeless and depressed.

Obsessive Compulsive Disorder (OCD): (*Obsession* is mental preoccupation; *compulsion* is driven behavior)

Ritualistic behavior and/or overpowering thoughts rule their lives. Minor symptoms include being "perfectionist" or "anal." Orderliness and perfectionism suppress flexibility and efficiency.

They are preoccupied with details, rules, lists, and schedules, and organization interferes with task completion. They avoid making decisions for fear of making mistakes.

Caught in details, they miss the big picture. Excessive devotion to work without leisure activity is characteristic, as is reluctance to delegate without exact compliance. They are conscientious workers, but not team players, considering others incompetent or careless.

The OCD often sets unreasonably high standards for themselves as well as others, and is highly critical when such expectations are not met. They are inflexible about morality, values, and ethics, and are miserly, rigid, and stubborn. They lack emotional warmth and are stiff, formal, and serious.

The "neat freak" constantly sorts and arranges items, showing an extreme preoccupation with order. A misplaced sock, a spot on a shirt, a scrambled pile of papers or magazines, a picture tilted on a wall -- all must be immediately corrected to prevent uneasiness, or even anger.

The "control freak" must do an activity repetitively, and/or in a certain way. Don't step on a crack on the sidewalk; turn the lights on and off an exact number of times; check the door locks over and over.

Phobias may be magnified by OCD (comorbidity). Germophobes continually clean and wash their hands, and dread doorknobs, keyboards, handrails, and library books. They won't touch anyone, nor do they want to be touched. They wear gloves constantly to avoid germs and may not go out in public without covering their noses and mouths.

The Narcissistic Personality Disorder (NPD)

The Narcissism Checklist ("The smartest, most talented, all-around, best person in the world test"). This checklist is a combination from Albert J. Bernstein, Ph.D., and the DSM-IV. Five or more starred items from *1-*9 are key indicators.

*1. Displays arrogant, haughty behavior or attitude.

*2. Preoccupied with fantasies of unlimited success, fame, power, brilliance, beauty, or idealized love.

*3. Has a grandiose sense of self-importance, firmly convinced that he is better, smarter, more talented, or better looking than other people.

*4. Has a sense of entitlement; expects special treatment or automatic compliance with his expectations.

*5. Is a name dropper to imply his association with famous or important people.

*6. Is interpersonally exploitative, taking advantage of others to achieve his or her own goals.

*7. Lacks empathy, unwilling to recognize or identify with the feelings and needs of others.

*8. Belief that he is special and can only be understood by, or should associate with, other special or high-status people or institutions, and feels it's very important to live in the right place.

*9. Is often envious of others or believes others are envious of them, and their criticism of him is motivated by jealousy.

10. Has achieved more than most people his age.

11. Loves competition, but hates losing.

12. Only interested in what other people are thinking or feeling if he wants something from them.

13. Usually manages to be in a category by himself.

14. Feels put upon if asked to take care of his responsibilities to family, friends and coworkers.

15. Regularly disregards rules, or expects them to be changed because he is special.

16. Becomes irritated when others don't automatically do what he asks, even if compliance isn't a good idea.

17. Reviews sports, art, literature, and other's works by saying how he would have done it instead.

18. Rarely able to recognize his mistakes, and then the slightest error can precipitate a major depression.

19. Often insists that people who are better known than he are really not all that great.

20. Often complains of being mistreated or misunderstood.

21. Either loved or hated by other people.

22. Intelligent and talented in spite of his over-inflated self image.

A recent National Institute of Mental Health study reveals that 3% of the population aged over 65, and 10% of those in their 20s, exhibit narcissism which tends to peak in adolescence, but decline with age.

It is easy to confuse a narcissist with an extrovert. Both can display charm, self assurance, friendly demeanor, and humor. While an egotist may be "full of himself" (boastful, conceited, self-centered), and repeatedly uses self references ("I," "me," "myself," and "mine"), the narcissist is a con artist with an extreme sense of self-importance, but fragile self-esteem.

Arrogance, lying, conceit, and megalomania place the narcissist at the top of the self-worshipping ladder. While most people are willing to share blame for failure, narcissists will blame someone else.

Milder narcissists are happy, less stress-inclined, rarely depressed or anxious, and rate their well-being highly. They feel invulnerable, able to handle whatever life throws at them. Their extreme self-confidence seems charming and attractive, and they feel pretty good about themselves.

But they need validation of their self worth by being admired, the center of attention, not just liked, and they feel entitled to special treatment. If they don't receive these, they are easily offended, harboring grudges. Their relationships are unstable since few people can tolerate them for long.

They love the sound of their own voice, but there is something "off" about their presentation, as if they're playing a role which, in fact, they are. Often dramatic, they may emphasize their haughty presence with, smiling and bowing, and colorful self-adornment.

To dominate, they are more argumentative, curse more, and use more sexual language than their modest counterparts. They brag, refocus discussion topics, are unable to engage in teamwork, make exaggerated hand movements, expansive arm gestures, talk loudly, and show disinterest by "glazing over" when others are speaking.

If that sounds like the 2016 presidential campaign, it's no coincidence.

Most people secretly think they're better than other people – more dependable, smarter, friendlier, harder-working, less-prejudiced, and even better lovers. As one researcher whimsically stated, "80% of people think they're better than average.

The narcissist regards others as mere instruments of gratification, and every interaction either reaffirms his worth or casts doubt on his vulnerable shell. Such unrealistic demands cause distress and social impairment. He is preoccupied with receiving awe, respect, admiration, attention, or even fear. This feedback is known as narcissistic supply (NS).

While pretending to be an expert, his knowledge is typically superficial, and he rages when contradicted or criticized.

Their grandiose, self-important narrative may exaggerate, or even fabricate, their achievements. They are obsessed with fantasies of unlimited power, success, fame, brilliance, beauty, and sexual performance.

They name-drop well-known individuals as personal friends and associates, and adopt as their own the experiences and accomplishments of others.

Malignant narcissism is more pathological, exhibiting paranoia, aggression, and sadism. He lacks empathy and is hurtful and destructive.

If he is humiliated, he reacts with indignation and often rage, blaming others for his explosive behavior, accusing them of provoking him. He believes that they should be punished for their misbehavior, and expects their apologies to be humiliating.

Situational narcissism is prevalent among high profile performers who crave the spotlight. They are often gifted and contribute to society as artists, authors, political leaders, business leaders, radio and TV commentators, or entertainers who enjoy basking in the limelight.

Their anger and frustration over lack of recognition of their greatness is often exemplified by public fits of indignation or rage. Examples include actors Alec Baldwin, Russell Crowe, Mel Gibson, and talk-show hosts Rush Limbaugh and Glenn Beck.

A psychologist observed that "Narcissism isn't too dissimilar from a compulsive behavior that gives the 'user' a high despite the fallout with others. This helps explain Charlie Sheen, most of the rest of Hollywood, and about 60% of everyone running for office."

The artificiality of "stardom" causes psychological harm to inexperienced youths whose televised singing, dancing, and beauty competitions breed unrealistic illusions of success, talent, and fame which are soon dashed by reality.

Religious narcissists include clergymen, evangelists, and cult leaders who profess to follow God because that association confers authority upon them. Preying upon their gullible flocks who provide continuous NS, they may humiliate and chastise their followers and abuse them financially, spiritually, and physically.

The religious narcissist seemingly merges with God by obeying His commandments and instructions, and communicating with Him. Conversely, he may even defy God since the bigger the narcissist's enemy, the more grandiose the narcissist feels. Examples include Charles Manson and Reverend Jim Jones of the People's Temple'

The Narcissist in Business

Many successful companies are run by narcissists full of confidence and charisma; they may be salesmen, entrepreneurs, surgeons, and other ego-intensive, highly-competitive professionals. So how do you deal with a narcissistic boss?

1. Butter him up, inviting his participation in matters which are overburdening. "Can we start next week? Without your guidance, we're lost on tough stuff like this."

2. Let him be the center of attention; some do well when all eyes are on them as they picture their glory. Stage fright is not an issue for these megalomaniacs. However, since narcissists' self-confidence has no basis in reality, they are often poor performers.

3. Make it clear to him from the beginning what you expect in return but remember, to the narcissist, it's all about him, and he won't play fair. If you do your job, at least you'll be compensated for it.

4. Don't cross him; a narcissist can act like an aggressive, cornered animal if they feels threatened. They don't want proof that they aren't special or getting enough respect. If you dare to criticize a narcissist, do it gently.

The Narcissist as a partner

Most anyone can be seduced by the narcissist because our society admires take-charge personalities. But narcissists make lousy partners. Their initial self-confidence and charm are very appealing, but their over-concern about their appearance and their ability to turn the charm on and off at will soon become apparent.

They are users who shun commitment and cheat since romantic relationships are just another way to pump up their own self-image. Narcissists look for mates with very high social status, good looks, or acknowledged success to complement their own inflated self image.

If your partner has had a string of relationships, constantly talks about how people admire him, and is easily angered when he doesn't get what he wants, he's a narcissist.

As one reporter observed, "If narcissists would simply date each other, each could have a self-confident, impressive and shallow mate, leaving the rest of us in peace."

The Cause and the Cure

Genetics may play a role, and overly-permissive parents who lavish their children with endless praise, thus depriving them of a normal coping mechanism in the real world, may also contribute.

If you think you're the greatest, why would you want to change? Narcissists most often show up for counseling with a spouse or relative who is having trouble with them, or they show up because of feelings of emptiness.

Antisocial Personality Disorder (APD)
The psychopath and the sociopath

"He will choose you, disarm you with his words, and control you with his presence. He will delight you with his wit and his plans. He will show you a good time, but you will always get the bill. He will smile and deceive you, and he will scare you with his eyes. And when he is through with you – and he will be through with you – he will desert you, taking with him your innocence and your pride. You will be left much sadder but not a lot wiser, and for a long time you will wonder what happened and what you did wrong." (From *Without Conscience - The Disturbing World of the Psychopaths among Us* by Dr. Robert Hare)

News item: December 19, 2010, Brazil: At the height of a happy wedding party, the new groom announced to the crowd that he had a surprise for them. He revealed that he was a sociopath who had fooled everyone, and then he shot and killed his new bride, his best man, and himself.

APD is an aggregate classification which includes sociopathy and psychopathy, and is occasionally called malignant narcissism.

"Primary" psychopaths display aggressive narcissism like arrogance, callousness, manipulativeness, and lying, whereas "secondary" psychopaths display mostly impulsivity, boredom proneness, irresponsibility, and lack of long-term goals.

Psychopaths are thought to have more hereditary causes, while sociopaths may be environmental. Cause is still the subject of considerable debate.

These stone-cold, egocentric individuals show a complete and utter disregard for the rights of others and the rules of society. There's really no effective treatment for them other than locking them up where they can't talk their way out.

They are natural-born predators who satisfy their lust for power and control by charm, manipulation, intimidation, and violence, and may kill for no apparent reason. They are considered criminals in all cultures except frontier or warlike societies where they become heroes, patriots, or leaders.

Serial killers and mass murderers

99% of serial killers are psychopaths, 95% of whom are men, and most of their victims are women. Psychopathic men commit three times the number of violent crimes than female psychopaths. They commonly display social isolation, schizophrenia, delusion, and paranoia. They avoid intimacy and are generally unsociable, blaming their problems on others and seeking to resolve their issues by an onslaught against those whom they perceive as rejecting and belittling them.

One in five violent offenders is a psychopath, characterized by a distinctive organization of the brain network that is used to learn from punishment and from rewards. These brain regions are involved in the processing of pro-social emotions such as guilt, embarrassment, moral reasoning, and empathy.

Offenders are reward driven and have difficulty learning from punishment to change their behavior. They have higher rates of recidivism, and don't benefit from rehabilitation programs.

Common criminals are hyper-responsive to threat, quick-tempered, and aggressive, while psychopaths have a very low, cold response to threats, and their aggression is premeditated.

Inside the mind of a mass murderer

While some murders may be psychotic and out of touch with reality, psychopaths are fully aware of what they are doing and plan carefully to inflict as much damage as possible to prevail over what they think has been a wrong committed against them, thus ruining them in some way, so murder is a justified recourse.

The depth of their rage occupies them continuously as they plot their revenge, revisiting the proposed location and practicing every detail. After their attack, they have no remorse and would commit the crime again, wishing they could cause more pain.

PET scans, functional MRI, head scans, chemical imbalances, and backgrounds have been studied, yet no one can predict with certainty who will become a mass murderer.

Anatomically, 94% of psychopaths reveal an asymmetrical hippocampus of the brain. A majority also displayed a larger but thinner corpus callosum.

Nearly 75% of APDs show early, lasting alcoholism and 50% abuse other drugs. Depression and suicide attempts in APD are about 5% – five times the general population. Violent behavior by APDs gradually tapers off in their 50s as they grow lonely and depressed.

Why don't these unhappy people simply kill themselves instead of multiple innocents?

The more victims, the more misery they can cause in retribution for what they think they have suffered. The tactic is shock and awe.

Therapy sessions

Psychopaths love to intellectualize with their interpretation of rules, but cannot handle cognition and emotion. When interviewed about their crime, they tend to imply that it had to be done, using words like "because," "since," and "so that."

They refer twice as much to physical needs like food, sex, or money than do non-psychopaths who refer to social needs like family, religion, and spirituality.

When institutionalized, they will attempt to escape, create a nuisance and a danger to staff, be a disruptive influence on other patients or inmates, and fake symptoms to get transferred, bouncing back and forth between institutions.

PET scans of murderers show that brain activity in the prefrontal cortex is lower than normal, a condition that is associated with risk taking, rule breaking, aggression, impulsivity, and violence. Their lack of compassion and empathy is like those with frontal lobe injuries.

TEN MYTHS ABOUT SCHOOL SHOOTINGS
A 2002 study of 37 attacks (U.S. Secret Service and U.S. Department of Education)

1. *"He didn't fit the profile"* There isn't one except they are male. They commonly fit the stereotypes of innocent students in regard to dress, race, family relationships, and achievement.

2. *"He just snapped"* Rarely are such acts sudden and impulsive. They plan and they gather weapons.

3. *"No one knew"* Before most attacks, someone else – a friend, classmate, or family member (but rarely an adult) – was aware of his plan. 80% told at least one person, 50% two or more. They expressed anger or violence in their writings, and were hostile toward teachers and classmates.

4. *"He hadn't threatened anyone"* Most attackers don't threaten, and most threateners don't attack.

5. *"He was a loaner"* The majority of attackers were in the mainstream, active in sports, clubs, and other activities, and even had girlfriends. Only 25% hung out with fringe groups.

6. *"He was crazy"* Only 10% were diagnosed with a mental disorder, and drug use was uncommon. However, most attackers had a history of suicidal thoughts or attempts, or long-term depression or desperation.

7. *"If the police had only shown up sooner or we had metal detectors"* Metal detectors have not deterred students committed to killing themselves or others. The Columbine killer fired his 50 rounds in under three minutes.

8. *"He'd never touched a gun"* Most had, and usually at home.

9. *"We did everything we could to help him"* Most shooters felt bullied, mocked, or injured by their peers, and had sought unsuccessfully for intervention by administrators or teachers.

Desperate for social engagement, they are characteristically shy, socially withdrawn, often mocked and humiliated by their peers. A resident police officer, anonymous tip line, and zero bullying tolerance would help.

10. *"School violence is rampant"* It's extremely rare, although it is on the increase, now averaging about 4 incidents per year in the nation's 100,000 schools. 2012 was particularly high (7 incidents) with multiple victims compounding this impression.

APD or Narcissism? It's the magnitude of the pathology

(1) APDs are usually unwilling or unable to control impulses. Narcissists may exhibit self control.

(2) APDs lack empathy, compassion, conscience, guilt, remorse, and usually anxiety as well. Narcissists may display some feelings and empathy toward others, and feel initial guilt for misconduct, but they immediately rationalize their behavior and shift the blame.

(3) APDs rarely form long-term, interpersonal relationships. Narcissists often do.

(4) APDs totally disregard society's rules, laws, ethics, morals and conventions, and brag about their infractions. Narcissists recognize the conventions of society and don't intentionally cause harm.

The APD's continuous display of chronic conduct disorder under age 15 grows into an adult disregard for, and violation of, the rights of others which may develop into crime and violence.

APDs are not psychotic and are capable of rational thinking. They know what society calls right and wrong, but choose their non-compliant behavior; therefore, they are not eligible for an insanity defense.

Profile: Rather than the sinister characters on TV crime shows who stalk their victims, the majority are successful, adapted, and non-violent. They seem rather normal as relatives, friends, co-workers, neighbors, or other acquaintances. Fewer than half of them have significant criminal records.

Many psychopathic traits like fearlessness, confidence, charisma, lack of empathy, and persistent focus are actually attributes in professions like surgery.

Male APDs are likely to emphasize intellect, power, aggression, money, and social status. Females are more likely to emphasize feminine stereotypes with looks, charm, sexuality, homemaking, and child rearing.

Despite all their outward bravado, many APDs describe themselves as empty, dark and void.

Hand gestures are used excessively by APDs, perhaps to help integrate their fragmented thinking as they typically change subjects or go off on tangents, disjointing their story line. This erratic, superficial thinking often causes slips of the tongue and the making up of words (neologisms), abbreviations, and sayings. They commonly avoid direct, thought-out responses to questions, preferring pat answers.

Statistics: A 2004 poll of 43,000 Americans revealed that 3.6% -- 1 in every 30 -- show APD tendencies (3:1 men to women), although they are not all diagnosed APD. They are twice as often found in inner cities than in small towns or rural areas. It is estimated that there are 30-50 active serial killers in the U.S. at any time.

APD tendencies are shown by up to 75% of prison inmates, but only 10-15% of them are psychopathic (15%-25% of the men and 7%-15% of the women). The majority of all violent crimes, including nearly half of the murders of on-duty law-enforcement officers, and mass murders, are committed by APDs. Serial pedophiles are also suspect.

The real-life Hannibal (The Cannibal) Lecter (*Silence of the Lambs*) was Britain's Robert Maudsley who bashed in the skull of a fellow prison inmate and ate his brain with a spoon.

Historically we've had Charles Manson, Ted Bundy, Jeffrey Dahmer, Gary Gilmore, David Berkowitz, Richard Kuklinski (The Iceman), John Wayne Gacey Jr., Dennis Rader (The BTK Killer—bind, torture, kill), Edward Teach (Blackbeard the pirate), William Bonney (Billy the Kid), John Dillinger, Reverend Jim Jones (Jonestown), David Koresh (Branch Davidians).

Gary Ridgeway (The Green River Killer) holds the U.S. record for serial killing 48 prostitutes within 20 years.

Former world-class APD tyrants responsible for the needless deaths of more than 100 million people include Germany's Adolph Hitler, China's Mao Tse-tung, Russia's Josef Stalin, Cambodia's Pol Pot, and Iraq's Saddam Hussein.

Rearing a Psychopath

In a recent year, 29 children under age 14 committed homicides in the U.S. One of these was Christian Fernandez, born to a 12-year-old mother who was sexually assaulted. He was found as a naked and dirty two-year old wandering a Florida street as his caretaker grandmother was holed up with cocaine in a messy motel room.

By age eight he had been sexually assaulted by his father and his cousin, and beaten by his stepfather. He had also killed a kitten and simulated sex acts with other students at school.

He once told a counselor, "You got to suck up feelings and get over it."

At age 11, left alone at home with his two half brothers, he sexually assaulted the five-year old and broke the two-year-old's leg. Two weeks later, left alone with them again, he beat the two-year-old to death.

Upon returning home and finding the dying child, his grandmother looked up "unconsciousness" on line, then spent the next 8-1/2 hours texting friends. She was sentenced to 30 years in prison for aggravated manslaughter.

During Christian's prison interviews, he openly discussed his life and was unemotional while detailing his crimes.

Childhood precursors

APD is not normally diagnosed in children or adolescents, often by law. Psychopathic tendencies are instead diagnosed as conduct disorder which fails to consider the traits of egocentricity and lack of remorse, empathy, or guilt. It has been estimated that approximately 30%-40% of ADHD and conduct-disorder children would test positive for APD.

Same-sex identical twins are more likely to exhibit psychopathic behavior than fraternal twins. If diagnosed as callous-unemotional ("CU") children, they display extreme antisocial behavior – fighting, bullying, lying, cheating, and stealing.

Precursor traits (The first three are "red flags"):

1. An extended period of bedwetting past the preschool years not due to any medical problem.

2. Precocious sadism, usually profound animal abuse.

3. Pathological, deliberate setting of destructive fires with utter disregard for the property and lives of others Punishment does not modify their behavior; consequently, parents usually

give up and the behavior worsens. (*Note: Playing with matches is normal for preschoolers*).

   * Lying, often without apparent reason, beyond a child's normal impulse not to be punished. These lies are so extensive it is often impossible to separate lies from truth.

   * Theft and truancy.

   * Aggression toward peers, not necessarily physical, such as getting others into trouble or a campaign of psychological torment.

Parental contributors

Mother exposed to deprivation or abuse as a child

Mother shows a tendency toward isolation

Mother cannot maintain a stable emotional connection with the child

Father transient, or the family migrates frequently

Common traits among APD children

Low birth weight or birth complications

Emotional hyposensitivity

Low sensitivity to pain

Hyperactivity

Failure to make eye contact when touched

Absence of fear of strangers

Low frustration tolerance

Transient psychotic episodes

Sense of omnipotence

Easily distracted

Transient relationships

Cruelty toward others and animals

Inability to recognize sad or fearful facial expressions or sad vocal tone.

THE CORPORATE APD

Professions which require human connection, deal with feelings, and don't offer much power, are not attractive to the psychopath, nor would he do well there. In contrast, power positions which require an ability to make objective, clinical decisions divorced from feelings are just right for the psychopath. He is likely to score at least six of the following traits:

1. Comes across as smooth, polished and charming
2. Turns most conversations around to a discussion about him
3. Discredits or puts others down in order to build up his own image and reputation
4. Lies with a straight face to his co-workers, customers or business associates
5. Considers people he has outsmarted or manipulated as stupid
6. Is opportunistic, ruthless, hating to lose and playing to win
7. Comes across as cold and calculating
8. Acts in an unethical or dishonest manner
9. Creates a power network which he uses for personal gain
10. Shows no regret for making decisions that negatively affect the company, shareholders or employees

Psychopath-attractive professions: CEO, lawyer, TV/Radio personality, surgeon, journalist, police officer, clergyman, chef, civil servant.
Non-psychopath-attractive professions: Nurse, therapist, doctor, caretaker, craftsperson/artist, beautician, charity worker, teacher, accountant.

Dr. Robert Hare's Psychopathy Checklist (abridged)

This time-honored test must be applied by a qualified technician, and includes in-depth interviews with the subject, family, acquaintances, business associates, police, social workers, and others. It is shown here with abbreviated clarifications.

DIRECTIONS: For each trait, score 2 if the subject matches fully, 1 if partially, or 0 if not at all. At least three of the highly-indicative, bold-numbered characteristics must be present. A total score above 25 suggests strong psychopathic tendencies.

1. Unstable, predatory relationships:

APDs tend to become involved with unstable partners; one study revealed that 75% of female felons had married APDs. Women who are attracted to male APDs are often hysteric or histrionic and feel empowered when attached to the APD; or they may be sado-masochistic, wanting to dominate or be dominated.

They live a "predatory" lifestyle, often attracting women by bragging, bravado, and lying to bolster their image, and feigning false emotions to simulate empathy.

To manipulate a woman, he will choose someone gullible, but to destroy a woman, he will choose one who can see through him. He will play mind games with her, instilling hope, and then betray her to destroy that hope.

Most often he will attack her self-esteem by accusing and questioning her honesty, fidelity, sanity, judgment. He may leave without a word after he has done as much damage as possible to make the victim feel like a punished child.

Divorcing an APD can be extremely dangerous; since his entire goal is to keep her under control to build up his low self-esteem, he may try to bleed his wife as dry as possible, or cause harm to their children.

Female APDs flaunt their gender, a charming "southern belle" schemer who appears to be a pitiful damsel in emotional distress, luring her target's protector/provider instincts with her sexuality. But when her mask comes off, she is cunning, ruthless, predatory, and loveless.

APDs frequent singles bars, social clubs, resorts, cruise ships, and foreign airports looking for lonely or homesick victims eager for excitement or companionship. Two may pair up like Leopold and Loeb, and the Menendez brothers, one being a "talker" and the other a "doer."

2. Manipulation and control:

The APD views everything and everyone as an object; preoccupation with weapons, money, goods, and people (viewed as objects), is a classic hallmark. They spend their lives seeking power through money and material goods, and by manipulation of people. They are driven by a need to prove their superiority while suspicious of others who may harm or humiliate them.

Deception is used to cheat, con, or defraud. They gravitate toward professions which guarantee abundant narcissistic supply. Failing that, they exert their power for fear and obedience.

An APD professional can masterfully fake his abilities and credentials, ascending to regional and national leadership roles during social distress like wars, economic breakdown, epidemics, and political conflict.

Most people are instinctively trusting, and are incredulous to discover that an acquaintance, or even a powerful and reputable individual like a CEO or political leader could be a psychopath.

They can inflict considerable damage in positions of power like lawyers, politicians, military heroes, trade union leaders, teachers, journalists, evangelists and cult leaders, unscrupulous businessmen, physicians and psychotherapists, hype-prone stock brokers, and boiler-room operators.

Criminal types may be serial killers, organized crime leaders, terrorists, rapists, thieves, con men and scammers, gangsters, child and spouse abusers, pimps, sadists, white-collar criminals, biker gang members, drug barons, and professional gamblers.

The APD must be in absolute control, often suspicious and paranoid. He backstabs his way to high position, ruthlessly abusing his power, showing bad judgment, placing others in precarious or failure situations. Those who see through the arrogance and perceive the empty shell are subject to elimination. The retribution can be brutal if the APD happens to be the boss.

The APD seems unable to believe that people have valid opinions different from theirs. Inferior, unworthy humans need to be convinced, punished, or extinguished. There can be only one winner.

On-line "cyberpaths" invent a persona to prey on confused, helpless, gullible, sympathetic, vulnerable targets. The unwillingness of an on-line correspondent to meet in person or talk on the telephone is a giveaway.

3. Pathological lying: They are pathological, unskilled liars, often for the sheer pleasure of it ("duping delight"), even if it's outrageously unbelievable, inconsistent and contradictory. They may use aliases, or just con others. If they forget the lies they've told and are caught, they simply deny the inconsistency and change their stories, often confusing the listener. If you try to pin him down, he will avoid answering your questions directly.

4. Arrogance: The APD is self-impressed by his grandiose demeanor, coming across as a self-assured, opinionated, cocky braggart. Despite frequent failure, he views himself as an important, entitled, disdainful and patronizing, superior being who is justified in living according to his own rules.

5. Absence of remorse or guilt: APDs are cold, contemptuous, inconsiderate, and tactless. They lack empathy for the losses and suffering of others, and even show disdain for their victims.

Usually they have handy excuses for their behavior and may deny that it even happened, feigning remorse if they are caught.

6. Superficial, exaggerated charm: Charismatic APDs tend to be smooth, charming, fast talking, persuasive liars, the life of the party – intelligent, talented, captivating, verbally fluent.

They are entertaining and convincing conversationalists and storytellers, apparently familiar with sociology, psychiatry, medicine, psychology, philosophy, poetry, literature, art, or law.

But they usually won't let you get a word in edgewise, flitting from topic to topic to avoid depth.

7. Need for constant stimulation: With an excessive need for stimulation and easily bored, APDs often fail to finish tasks.

8. Lack of emotion: Primary APDs do not respond to punishment, apprehension, stress, or disapproval, and seem unable to experience genuine emotion or response to kindness.

Normal experimental subjects show mounting anxiety when anticipating an electric shock; APDs don't even sweat.

Emotionally-charged words like "rape" and "cancer" trigger brain-wave jolts in normal subjects, APDs show no response.

The APD may refer to himself and others in the third person or as a machine. He has no familiarity with personal values or feelings and takes no interest in tragedy, grief, or the humanity found in art and literature, and isn't moved by beauty, ugliness, love, horror, or even humor.

He may say he understands without knowing that he doesn't understand. As psychologists J. H. Johns and H. C. Quay say, the psychopath "knows the words but not the music." Even that statement would be meaningless to the APD.

In the mildest cases, bordering narcissism, some APDs can cry real tears and are even emotionally "touched" by sunsets, laughing children, and beautiful music, but without the depth of feeling of mainstream society. But by reading a lot, and communicating with people who experience emotions, the APD can predict and adjust to people's behavior.

9. Impulsiveness and risk taking: Impetuous, APDs are incapable of considering the consequences of foolhardy, reckless behavior, often endangering themselves and others.

10. Refusal to accept blame: Absence of conscientiousness and sense of duty causes failure to accept responsibility; thus, they shift the blame (projection).

11. Teenage misbehavior: APD traits appear by adolescence, and are legally diagnosable by age 18. These traits include a pervasive disregard for rules; violation of the rights of others; torturing or killing animals (even a general dislike of animals); vandalism and fire setting; frequent lying and cheating; repetitive truancy; theft; bullying and fighting with school mates; precocious sexual experimentation; glue sniffing and alcohol use; immunity to pain in themselves and indifference to pain in others; unresponsiveness to discipline; defiance of parental and teacher authority; and running away from home

12. Parasitic, freeloading lifestyle: Intentional exploitation of, and financial dependence on, others.

13. Poor temper control: "Distempered" APDs, if challenged, easily fly into a red-faced rage or even a frenzy resembling an epileptic fit. They have low tolerance for frustration; when things are not going their way, they are brash, arrogant, and resentful. They perceive casual remarks as attacks, thereby justifying their outbursts as a reasonable defense.

14. Sexual promiscuity: Numerous brief, superficial affairs with casually-selected sexual partners are common, as is maintaining several simultaneous relationships, and attempting to coerce others into sexual activity.

Sexual attitudes are inappropriate or perverse; they tend to say sexually-inappropriate things to people they barely know, bragging about their sexuality and numbers of partners they've had.

15. Belligerent bullying: APDs are often irritable, confrontational, and intimidating, often resulting in fights or assaults. Many people report the particular stare of the APD – an intense, relentless gaze described as "predatory" or "reptilian," as if he is directing all of his intensity and hatred through his eyes. One wife described this malevolent foreboding as a feeling of "being eaten" by her APD husband.

16. Lack of realistic planning: Long-term plans and goals are elusive to the APD; they lead a nomadic, impulsive, aimless existence, living in the present, unable to plan for the future.

17. Lack of empathy and conscience: Although APD is a composite of symptoms, the absence of empathy, conscience, compassion, and guilt feelings is central.

18. Irresponsibility: APDs repeatedly fail to meet obligations and commitments, ignore bills, default on loans, perform sloppy work, are absent or late to work, break promises, and fail to honor contractual agreements, disregarding the consequences.

19. Generally poor behavior: For all the previous descriptors, APDs are often called obnoxious or hateful. Nearly half of them have significant and frequent arrest records, mostly with business associates, traffic offenses, and severe marital difficulties like domestic violence.

They tend to invade people's space; if you are alone in a room, they might suddenly intrude and give you the stare, watching your reaction. Some women misread that look-over as sexuality.

INTERVIEWING A PSYCHOPATH

Maintaining rapport is important to encourage the subject to relax and vent. Until rapport has been established, address the subject as Mister or Misses.

A psychopath is often highly intelligent, cunning, and perceptive – don't react emotionally to anything he might say.

Your professional attire communicates authority, and the psychopath wants to communicate with the upper echelon.

Psychopaths like to be the center of attention and they want everyone to know how smart they are. To encourage him to talk, use open-ended questions as though you are learning from him:

"What would you do? Can you help me figure this out?"

If given information about a crime, he may volunteer evidence or even confess, possibly in the third person ("Then he got into her car…").

If challenged or caught in a lie, he may attempt to shock the interrogator or become aggravated, verbally attacking the interrogator, or he may shed crocodile tears and display emotional theatrics.

Their lack of stress response may allow them to do well on polygraph tests and even convince an interrogator of their innocence.

TAKE-HOME POINTS

Typically, psychology students recognize many symptoms in themselves and in others, but occasional off-beat thoughts and quirkiness are normal. To be pathological, they must be pervasive, and a valid diagnosis requires training and experience.

While it's true that narcissists and psychopaths can display charisma and leadership, not all charismatic people or strong leaders are narcissists; they may be sincerely altruistic.

Movies and television depictions of psychological pathologies are maximized and dramatized to draw viewership. Mean characters are cast as is sadistic, psychopathic, serial killers. But in real life such predators are very rare; that's why they make the news.

Having a psychopathic trait doesn't make someone a psychopath, which is a syndrome of anti-social traits.

The inexperience of youth presents a wide range of behavior which narrows with maturity.

There's a huge gap between a symptom and a diagnosis. Having a cough doesn't mean you have lung cancer, and having occasional weird thoughts, or displaying an inappropriate action, doesn't make anyone a mental case.

On-line resource for personality disorders:
http://www.healthyplace.com/personality-disorders/malignant-self-love/personality-disorders-toc/menu-id-1469/
www.dsm5.org